Squirrel Rescue

by Anna Leske
Illustrated by Lane Gregory

PEARSON

Scott
Foresman

Editorial Offices: Glenview, Illinois • Parsippany, New Jersey • New York, New York
Sales Offices: Needham, Massachusetts • Duluth, Georgia • Glenview, Illinois
Coppell, Texas • Sacramento, California • Mesa, Arizona

squirrel

When Papá pulled into the driveway, Félix and Inéz ran to meet him.

"Papá!" they yelled. "Come quickly! We have something to show you."

Papá followed the children into the backyard. He saw a half-grown squirrel at the bottom of the gully. The squirrel was limping painfully back and forth.

"Mamá says not to touch him," Inéz said, "but he's all alone and he's hurt. We have to do *something*, don't we?"

2

police car

Papá looked at the children.

"Mamá is right!" he said. "It's best to leave wild animals alone. That little squirrel might bite you, or he might be sick. You might hurt him more if you pick him up."

Papá thought for a moment. Then he said, "Stay away from the squirrel, but keep him in sight. I think I know someone who can help."

Then he scrambled back to his police car and drove away.

cage

When Papá returned, a woman carrying a small cage was with him.

"This is Mrs. Jackson," Papá said. "She and I have worked together before. She and her son are wildlife rehabilitators. That means she has studied how to help injured wild animals. It's against the law for most people to keep wild animals, but Mrs. Jackson has permission."

Mrs. Jackson watched the limping squirrel thoughtfully. Then she said, "Let's see what I can do to help this little creature."

---

wildlife rehabilitators: people who help injured animals return to a healthy, normal life in the wild

blanket

Mrs. Jackson moved slowly toward the squirrel, murmuring soft, comforting words. She picked it up carefully with a small blanket and put it into the cage.

Mrs. Jackson turned to the children. "Would you like to come to my house tomorrow to see how this little guy is doing? Your dad knows where I live."

wheelchair

The next day Félix and Inéz rode their bikes to Mrs. Jackson's house. A teenage boy answered the door.

"I'm Dean," he said, "and you must be the ones who found the squirrel. Come with me, and you can see him."

Dean rolled toward a sunny room at the back of the house. Félix and Inéz followed.

There were several cages in the room. Most of the cages were empty, and the children saw the squirrel right away. One of its legs was shaved, and it still limped slightly. Otherwise it looked lively and happy.

"Mom took the squirrel to the vet right away. The vet fixed his leg, and he's old enough to live on his own, but we need to watch him for a while. Would you like to help care for him?"

Schedule

FEEDING	
Morning	Dean
Noon	Mom
Evening	Mom
Special	Dean
CLEANING	Dean
SHOPPING	Mom

Dean pointed to a schedule on the wall. It had spaces for feeding, cleaning, and shopping.

"When we have a lot of animals here," Dean said, "we are very, very busy. Some animals need to be fed several times a day. We can always use help with feeding and with cleaning the cages."

Félix and Inéz promised to come back every afternoon.

"We'd like to keep him as a pet," Inéz said. "May we take him home when he gets well?"

"It would not be right to keep him," Mrs. Jackson said. "A squirrel is a wild animal. Squirrels need to be free. They should follow their instincts and live with other squirrels. This squirrel would not be happy living as a pet."

Félix and Inéz were disappointed, but they didn't say anything.

9

For the next week, Félix and Inéz went to the Jackson house every day. As they worked, they learned about rehabilitating wild animals. Watching the squirrel, they began to understand what Mrs. Jackson meant about wild animals and instincts.

One day Mrs. Jackson took the squirrel's cage outdoors and put it under a shady tree. The children knew it was almost time to say good-bye.

The next day, Félix, Inéz, and the Jacksons met in the backyard. Dean opened the cage door.

At first the squirrel just sat there. Then it slowly walked out and sniffed an acorn on the ground. Next it scampered a little without limping at all. Finally it climbed a tree at the edge of the yard, looked at its human friends one last time, and scurried away.

Extend Language   Ways to Move

How many ways can a squirrel move? Here are a few. Can you think of more?

- *walk*—to move at a normal rate
- *scamper*—to run playfully
- *limp*—to walk with uneven steps
- *climb*—to move upward
- *scurry*—to take small, quick steps

"The squirrel looks happy," said Félix, "but I'm not. I'll miss him."

"We'll miss you and Dean too," added Inéz. "We've enjoyed learning about caring for animals."

"You don't have to miss us," Dean said with a smile. "More animals probably will arrive soon. We'll need more help then. And you two are a big help!"

The children smiled. They knew they could rehabilitate more animals in the future.